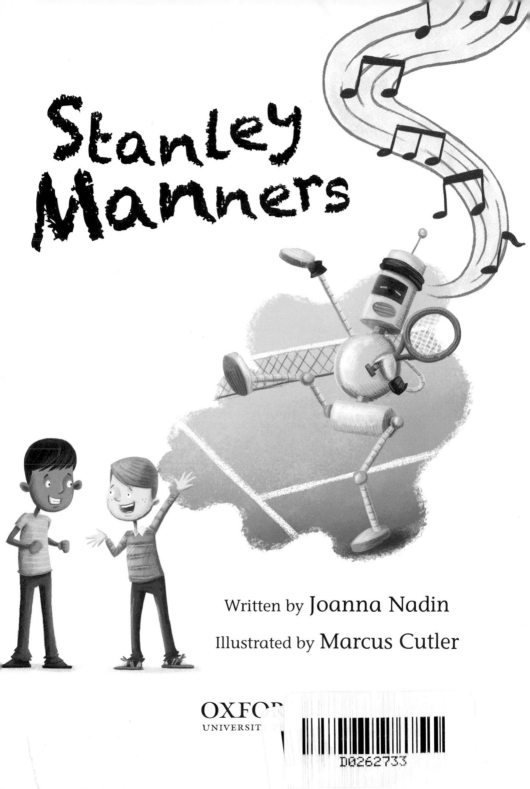

Stanley Manners

Written by **Joanna Nadin**

Illustrated by **Marcus Cutler**

OXFORD
UNIVERSIT

OXFORD
UNIVERSITY PRESS

Great Clarendon Street, Oxford, OX2 6DP, United Kingdom

Oxford University Press is a department of the University
of Oxford. It furthers the University's objective of excellence
in research, scholarship, and education by publishing
worldwide. Oxford is a registered trade mark of Oxford
University Press in the UK and in certain other countries

Text © Joanna Nadin 2015
Illustrations © Oxford University Press 2015

The moral rights of the author have been asserted

First published 2015

British Library Cataloguing in Publication Data
Data available

ISBN: 978-0-19-835675-2

10 9 8 7 6 5 4 3

Paper used in the production of this book is a natural, recyclable product
made from wood grown in sustainable forests. The manufacturing process
conforms to the environmental regulations of the country of origin.

Printed in China by Leo Paper Products Ltd

Acknowledgements

Series Advisor: Nikki Gamble
Designed by Ana Cosma
Illustrated by Marcus Cutler

Chapter 1
Big Beastly Lies

Stanley Manners told lies. Not just little white lies, but **big beastly whoppers**.

At breakfast he lied to his dad.

"Stanley, will you *please* stop fiddling with the spoon and eat your cereal?" said Dad.

"I can't," replied Stanley. "The spoon is stuck to my nose because I have magnetic super powers."

Which he hadn't.

At school he lied to Patsy Prendergast.

"I have a pony called Princess Pinkerton," boasted Patsy. "And she eats apples right out of my hand!"

"I have a dragon called Douglas," replied Stanley. "And it eats ponies."

Which he hadn't.
And it didn't.

At dinner he lied to his gran.

"I went to bingo today," said Gran, "and I won some money and a box of chocolates."

"I went to the moon," replied Stanley, "and I won a medal from the Queen."

Which he didn't.

Stanley didn't mean to tell lies, he just wanted life to be more exciting. But no one understood.

"Stop lying, Stanley," they all said. "It'll get you in **big** trouble one day."

But Stanley didn't listen. "It's not fair," he muttered to himself. "Grown-ups are always telling lies."

Which they were.

"Eat your crusts or your hair
won't curl," said Dad.

"If the wind changes, your face
will stay like that," said Gran.

Grown-ups even lied to each other.

"Does this dress suit me?" asked Gran.

"Absolutely," replied Dad. "You look as pretty as a picture."

Which she didn't.

Gran was the worst of all.

"If you wish hard enough," she said, "your wish will come true."

But it never did.

"It's not fair," Stanley repeated to himself. "If they can lie, why can't I?"

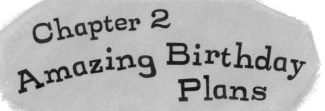

Chapter 2
Amazing Birthday Plans

Stanley's birthday was getting close
and he had invited his friends to his party.

"What presents are you
getting?" asked Raj
Chatterjee the day
before Stanley's party.
"I got a robot for
my birthday and
it can walk."

"I'm getting a gold
robot," replied Stanley.
"And it can walk, play
tennis and sing."

"What sort of cake will you have?" asked Elsie Atkins, who loved cake. "I had a chocolate one for my birthday party and it was taller than our teapot."

"Mine will be chocolate, cherry and banana flavour," replied Stanley. "And it will be taller than Mrs Bottomley." (Who was very tall indeed!)

"Will there be a conjuror?"
asked Ruby Hooper.
"I had a conjuror called
The Great Gregorio and
he was the best in town."

"I'm having *two* conjurors,"
replied Stanley. "And they're the
best in the whole wide world."

"Dad," said Stanley when he got home that day. "Please can I have a gold robot that walks, plays tennis and sings? And two conjurors who are the best in the whole wide world? And a cake that has three flavours and is two metres tall?"

"Of course you can," said Dad. "And why
don't I throw in a tap-dancing bear and a goose
that lays golden eggs, at the same time?"

"Thanks," said Stanley.

But he knew it was a lie.

"Never mind," said Gran before bed. "If you wish hard enough, your wish will come true."

"That," thought Stanley, "was the biggest lie of all."

Chapter 3
Happy Birthday, Stanley!

But on the morning of his birthday, Stanley lay in bed thinking. Maybe, he thought, just maybe, Gran hadn't been lying after all. Maybe if he did wish hard enough he could have a three-flavoured cake taller than Mrs Bottomley, the two best conjurors in the whole wide world and a gold robot that walks, plays tennis and sings.

So he wished and he
wished, harder than he had
ever wished for anything in
his life. Even harder than the
time he wished he could be
invisible so he wouldn't have
to go to the dentist.

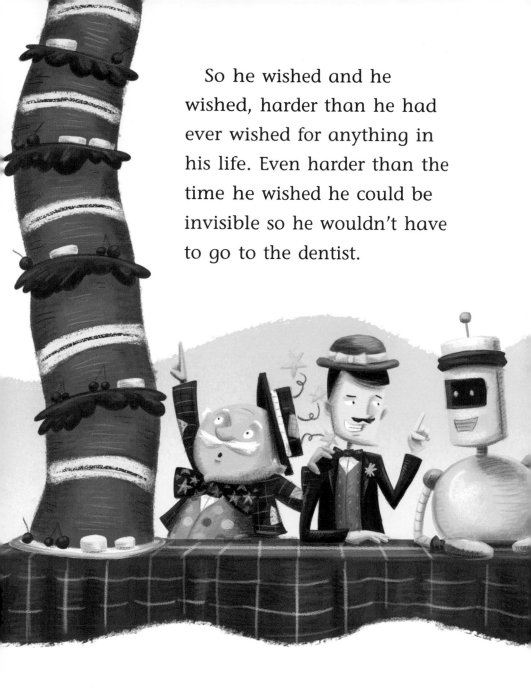

Then Stanley sprinted downstairs to open
his presents.

He got a book about bees from his dad,
a giant lollipop from his gran, and a hat from
Aunty Annie who lived in the countryside.

"Is that it?" asked Stanley, trying not to
sound disappointed.

"What were you expecting?" asked Dad.

"Umm, nothing," muttered Stanley.

"Don't you like your presents?" asked Gran.

"They're all absolutely ... wonderful," said Stanley.

That was already two big lies – and it was only half past eight.

"I don't think you wished hard enough," said Gran as they were cutting sandwiches into triangles for the party. "Otherwise, you'd have your robot after all."

"That's a *big, fat* lie," thought Stanley. "Honestly, she must think I'll believe anything!"

But he wished really hard again anyway.
Harder than he had wished earlier. Harder
than the time he wished for a flying monkey
and a hat made of cheese. He wished for
the robot and the conjurors and the cake.
He even wished for a pet dragon.

"Might as well," thought
Stanley, "because it's never
going to happen!"

Then Stanley sat on the doorstep and waited
for his friends.

Chapter 4
Unexpected Guests

Raj Chatterjee was the first to arrive. "Did you get your gold robot?" he asked excitedly.

"Umm, not yet," Stanley said hesitantly.

Patsy Prendergast showed up on her pony, Princess Pinkerton. "Where are the conjurors?" she asked. "I don't see one, let alone *two*. *Or* a dragon."

"Umm, they'll be here soon," muttered Stanley.

Elsie Atkins and Ruby Hooper came together.
"I can't wait for the cake!" Elsie exclaimed.
"I hope it really *is* taller than Mrs Bottomley,"
added Ruby.

"N—N—Nearly," stammered Stanley, with
a crooked smile. But inside he wasn't smiling.
Inside he felt sick.

"I should have cancelled the party," he whispered to Gran. "I should have said I had measles or mumps or something that makes all your hair fall out and your ears go purple."

Stanley was busy thinking of all the
illnesses he could pretend to have. He was
just imagining something that could make
his legs turn to jelly and his eyes spin around,
when he heard a loud noise.

"I am Marvin
the Marvellous," bellowed a deep voice.

"And I am Simon
the Splendiferous," announced another voice.

Stanley looked up to see two oddly dressed men standing in front of him, with silly hats, brightly coloured clothes, and bow ties that spun around and around.

"WOW!" said Stanley's friends.

Simon the Splendiferous clapped his hands and a gigantic cake appeared, topped with three kinds of icing, silver sprinkles and a cherry the size of a football.

"Oooh!" gasped Stanley's friends.

Marvin the Marvellous clapped his hands and a parcel appeared. Stanley quickly tore away the wrapping paper to find a gold robot that walked, played tennis and sang (although it was a bit out of tune).

"Aaah!" said Stanley's friends.

Marvin and Simon both clapped their hands and a giant cloud of smoke appeared. From inside the cloud came a strange growling noise.

"Eeek!" said Stanley's friends.

"What's **that?**" cried Stanley.

"That looks like it could be Douglas, your pet dragon!" said Gran as the smoke disappeared.

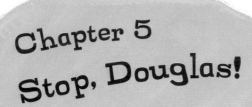

Chapter 5
Stop, Douglas!

"My *what*?" exclaimed Stanley.
"But I don't have a drag—"
                    Only he did.

Because there, right in front of him,
was an enormous orange dragon.

"Graaaaaar!"
roared the dragon.

Dad screamed and dived into the rose bushes.
Elsie Atkins yelped and hid behind a tree.
Raj Chatterjee wailed and shot up the tree.

"I'm not scared," said Ruby Hooper, folding her arms.

But the dragon stomped on the cake, sending the cherry flying straight into Ruby's face.

"Ouch!" she cried.

Next, the dragon whipped his tail around, smashing the gold robot to smithereens. Several pieces landed on Patsy Prendergast.

"Do something, Stanley!" she shrieked.

"Umm, over here, Douglas!" Stanley said, waving his giant lollipop at the dragon.

But Douglas didn't want a lollipop, not even a giant one. Douglas wanted something much bigger, much hairier and much more pony-like. Douglas wanted Princess Pinkerton!

"Stop!" yelled Patsy Prendergast as the dragon lumbered towards them.

"Stop!" yelled Simon the Splendiferous, and he clapped his hands together. But all he did was turn Raj's nose green.

"**Stop!**" yelled Marvin the Marvellous, and he clapped his hands together. But all he did was shower everyone with popcorn.

Douglas roared again, setting fire to a rose bush and scorching the garden furniture. Dad screamed again and ran into the shed.

But someone wasn't scared.

"Well, Stanley," said Gran calmly.
"You certainly got what you wished for."

"I'm sorry!" cried Stanley. "I didn't mean it.
I take it all back."

"All of it?" asked Gran.

Stanley watched as the terrifying dragon
stomped closer and closer to Princess Pinkerton.

"Yes!" he said quickly. "All of it!"

Chapter 6
The Biggest Wish of All

Stanley closed his eyes and made an absolutely enormous, gigantic, colossal wish. A wish so big he felt it tingle in his toes and tickle his nose as he wished it.

"Please," he said, "please make it all go away and I will never, never ever tell a lie again."

When Stanley opened his eyes he was astonished to see that the dragon had disappeared. So had the enormous cake, the two conjurors and the remains of the gold robot.

All that was left was a piece of Simon the Splendiferous's coat, which was caught on the rose bush.

"Is it time for lunch yet?" asked Elsie Atkins.
"I think it's time to go home," sighed Dad.
Which, amazingly, even
Patsy thought was a good idea.

At school on Monday, everything had gone back to how it was before. Patsy was back to boasting about her new poodle, Precious Pants. Elsie was back to dreaming about a cake taller than Mrs Bottomley, and Raj's nose was back to its usual colour.

But someone had changed. And that someone was Stanley. Because now, when he was asked a question, he always told the truth.

"What are you doing on Saturday, Stanley?"
asked Elsie Atkins.

"Tidying my bedroom,"
said Stanley.

"What's in your sandwich, Stanley?" asked
Ruby Hooper.

"Strawberry jam," said Stanley.

"If you could have one wish, what would it be?" asked the new boy, Matthew Mills.

"Oh," said Stanley, "I'd probably just wish for a new football."

"You're lying," muttered Matthew.

But Stanley just smiled and thought to himself, "Be careful what you wish for!"